Spelling Tricks and Rules for 3rd-4th Graders:
To Learn, Improve, & Have Fun with Spelling

For ages 8-9

(American English)

by
Joanne Rudling
from
www.howtospell.co.uk

Are you ready to learn some secrets and tricks to help your spelling?

Spelling Tricks and Rules for 3rd-4th Graders:
To Learn, Improve, & Have Fun with Spelling

ISBN: 9781082206801 (paperback)

Published by
How to Spell Publishing
www.howtospell.co.uk

All photos purchased from depositphotos.com, or royalty free from openclipart.org and pixabay.com.

Contents

Spelling improves if you:
→ study it
→ practice it
→ think about it
→ notice it
→ write it

Be a spelling detective and investigate peculiar spellings.

Introduction

Welcome to the wonderful world of spelling.

This book is full of **spelling tricks, rules,** and **fun tips** to help you understand, learn, and love spelling.

➔ If you feel like this about spelling, working through this book will make you feel like this.

Spelling is stupid!

➔ Do you have your colored pens and pencils ready?

➔ A spare piece of paper is good for trying out the writing exercises.

➔ Don't go crazy and race through this book; take your time and enjoy it.

➔ Enjoy the words, art, writing, and exercises.

➔ And remember, making mistakes is good if you learn from them, so don't get stressed about getting things wrong.

➔ If you don't want to write in this book, grab your favorite notebook and do all the exercises, writing, word art, and drawings in it.

Word Study

Be a spelling detective
study, notice, write

Please, remember that just because you've seen a word once doesn't mean you're going to be able to spell it. **You have to work on spelling and study it just like math, science, history, or any other subject.**

Spelling a word correctly happens when you **get to know a word** and become **friends with it**. Ways to do this include:

✓ knowing how it can change with **spelling rules**

✓ understanding how we can make it longer with prefixes and **suffixes**

✓ noticing the common letter patterns (also called letter strings)

✓ using memory tricks to help you spell it if it's a tricky word

Pro tip: ➔ **Use a dictionary if you don't understand a word.**

Using Memory Tricks to Remember Your Spelling

Do you want to know a secret?

You can use all sorts of **tricks** and **strategies** to **learn** and **remember** your **spelling**. For example, you can:

 ✓ See **words within words** (*piece of pie, add an address, my heart is in art*).

 ✓ See **vowels** (*remember, extreme, excellent, grammar, separate, opposite*).

 ✓ Notice the **root words**, prefixes and suffixes (*unusually, disappearing, unbelievable*).

 ✓ Use syllable breakdown (im-por-tant, ex-pe-ri-ment, Feb-ru-a-ry, Wed-nes-day).

 ✓ Spell with **rhymes** and **sentences** ("i before e except after a long c," *never believe a lie*).

 ✓ Use memory tricks to help you spell tricky spellings.

 ✓ Know **spelling rules** (drop the "e" — believe ➜ believing).

Good spellers use these strategies and memory tricks all the time, especially to remember difficult spellings. You might think some are fantastic, or some are stupid, but that's fine. Use what you like and what works for you.

➜Using memory tricks, **seeing words within words**, and noticing vowels are important methods because sometimes we forget spellings when we don't use them all the time, especially tricky spellings like *calendar, believe, address, separate.*

➜To help us figure out if it's *calander* or *calendar, adress* or *address, seperate* or *separate*, we can use some of the strategies above. We'll go into more detail about these in the book.

Pro tip: ➜ If you come up with your own **memory trick**, you'll remember it.
    Use whatever works for you to help you remember a spelling, no matter how crazy it is.

Word Art and Drawing Pictures

→ *Word art* and drawing pictures help you remember spellings.

→ Adding details to the letters — shading, doodling around the letters, or coloring in the vowels or difficult bits — can help you learn spellings.

It's *brrrr* in February.

→Your pictures & word art don't have to be perfect; just enjoy putting them down on paper.

→Do some word art for your name.

Spotting Vowels

➜ Spotting vowels is a great strategy, especially for dyslexics.
➜ Use colors to highlight the vowels.

excellent, remember, recent, sentence, therefore, extreme, center
believe, experience, experiment, exercise, complete, different, deceive
grammar, calendar, natural, separate, interest
decide, describe, medicine
opposite, position, potato/potatoes
difficult, division
museum

This is just one of many useful spelling strategies to help you. If you love it, or find it helpful, then please use it. You can use it in combination with the other strategies we're going to look at.

➜ **Do some word art for these words and use colors for the vowels.**

→ Sometimes, the meaning of a word can give us a clue to the vowel letter patterns:

beech or beach?

A b__ee__ch is a tr__ee__. / A b__ea__ch is by the s__ea__.

→ Use memory tricks for difficult vowel patterns: Color in the tricky vowels:

because — Bec**a**use you need to **a**lways **u**nderstand.   bec__ __se

believe — Do you bel**ie**ve **I** exist?   bel__ __ve

thought — I th**ou**ght **o**f y**ou**.   th__ __ght

build — Y**ou** and **I** b**ui**ld a house.   b__ __ld

Exercise

1. Can you guess these words without the vowels?
2. Now add the vowels.
3. Check on the next page to see if you're right.

r__m__mb__r,   r__c__nt,   s__nt__nc__,   c__nt__r,   __xtr__m__

gr__mm__r,   d__c__d__,   c__l__nd__r,   __pp__s__te

d__ff__c__lt,   d__ff__r__nt,   th__r__for__,   __nt__r__st

n__t__r__l,   s__p__r__t__,   m__d__c__n__,   __xp__r__ __nc__

Bec__ __se you need to __lways __nderstand.   I th__ __ght __f yó__.

Do you bel__ __ve __ __xist?   Yo__ and __ b__ __ld a house.

Answers

remember, recent, sentence, center, extreme,
grammar, decide, calendar, opposite,
difficult, different, therefore, interest,
natural, separate, medicine, experience.

Because you need to always understand.   I thought of you.

Do you believe I exist?   You and I build a house.

→ Rewrite these again in your notebook using different colors for the different vowels.

→ Get your friend or parent to give you a spelling test with these. Or record them and test yourself.

→ A words-within-words preparation exercise

Warning! Multiple choice exercises can really mess with your brain because they give you spelling alternatives which also look right!

Multiple choice exercises are only useful when you can use various tricks and strategies to help you, such as:

- using memory tricks
- understanding spelling rules
- knowing common letter patterns
- seeing vowels (We've just looked at this strategy.)

We'll look at these in more detail in the book.

→Look at these important words you will likely have to spell. Which is correct?

→ **Don't worry about making mistakes. Mistakes are fabulous** because you can learn from them, so be bold and choose the one you think is right — no stress because this is between you and me.

1. a. seperate
   b. separate

2. a. appear
   b. apear

3. a. different
   b. differant

4. a. beleive
   b. believe

5. a. calender
   b. calendar

6. a. business
   b. buisness

7. a. peculier
   b. peculiar

8. a. arguement
   b. argument

Answers

1. ~~a. seperate~~
   b. separate

2. a. appear
   ~~b. apear~~

3. a. different
   ~~b. differant~~

4. ~~a. beleive~~
   b. believe

5. ~~a. calender~~
   b. calendar

6. a. business
   ~~b. buisness~~

7. ~~a. peculier~~
   b. peculiar

8. ~~a. arguement~~
   b. argument

Remember, don't worry about making mistakes. In this book, you're going to learn how to spell these tricky spellings, and then use them in the writing sections.

➔ I know multiple choice exercises aren't as hard as spelling the words in a spelling test, so that's why it's important to practice these words in the writing sections in this book. Or get your friend or parent to do a spelling test with you.

➔ All the words in the exercise above have a small word inside them that you can use as a memory trick to help you spell them. Next, we're going to look at these words within words.

Words within Words

➜ Some of the strategies/memory tricks I'm going to discuss in this section are very good for remembering spellings. You might like some of these and want to use them, or you might not like some of them — that's fine. Use whatever helps you remember a spelling.

➜ Seeing words within words can help you remember the difficult bits of the word, the tricky letter patterns (-ie- or –ei-), the silent letters, double consonants, and which homophone is which.

Exercise

Can you see the **small word within** these tricky words?

For example, *believe* - when you don't tell the truth: <u>lie</u>

1. *separate* — an animal (a rodent) is in this word: _____

2. *business* — you can travel to work on this: _____

3. *peculiar* — someone who doesn't tell the truth is a _____

4. *position* — the opposite of stand is to _____

5. *argument* — you can chew this: _____

Pro tip: ➜ If you don't understand a word, use a dictionary.

12

➜ Seeing a small word within tricky words can help you spell them, especially if the "little" word is somehow related to the "big" word (check the words below to see what I mean).

Answers

1. bel**ie**ve — when you don't tell the truth: <u>lie</u>

2. sepa**ra**te — an animal (a rodent) is in this word: <u>rat</u>

3. **bus**iness — you can travel to work on this: <u>bus</u>

4. pecu**liar** — someone who doesn't tell the truth is a <u>liar</u>

5. po**sit**ion — the opposite of stand is to <u>sit</u>

6. ar**gum**ent — you can chew this: <u>gum</u>

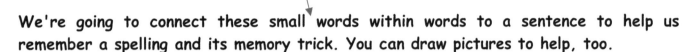

We're going to connect these small words within words to a sentence to help us remember a spelling and its memory trick. You can draw pictures to help, too.

➜ See the small word with the -ie- pattern in **believe**  and connect it to a sentence: *Never **bel**ie**ve** a lie.*

➜Write your memory tricks and do some *word art* for **believe**.

Remember to spot the vowels bel**ie**ve.
Do you believe **I** exist?
Bel**ie**ve **Eve** the alien.

➜ Can you think of your own **memory tricks** for these words within words? It doesn't matter how crazy your 'tricks' are as long as they help you remember the tricky spelling.

Write your memory tricks and do some *word art.*

➜ **separate**
See the rat in <u>sepa**ra**te</u>.
Sepa**ra**te **a** rat.
Spot the vowels too:
s**e**p**a**r**a**t**e**

➜ Work on the words you find difficult.   **Write your memory tricks and do some** *word art.*

➜ **heard**

  ear — hear — <u>heard</u>
Hear with your ear and learn.

➜ **appear/disappear**
There <u>appears</u> to be an app in my ear.

➜ disappear

➜ **business**
It's good <u>busi**ness**</u> to go by bus.

Careful, **busyness** means being very busy, very active — *School started and the busyness began.*

➜**position**
Sit in this <u>posi**tion**</u>.

➜**opposite**
I sit **oppo**s**ite** her.

➜ **argument**
argue but <u>arg**um**ent</u>
Don't chew gum in an arg**um**ent.
Argue ➜ drop the "e" when *arguing* and having an ***argument***.

➜**address**
add an <u>add**ress**</u>

→ **heart**

My <u>he</u>art is in art.

→ **peculiar**

He's a **pecul**iar liar.

Liar, liar, pants on fire — what a peculiar sentence!   He's a *familiar peculiar* liar.

→**calendar**

Len checks his <u>calendar</u> every day.

A **calen**dar is a list of dates.

→ **measurement**

Be sure to <u>mea</u>sure your **mea**sure**ments**.

→ **pressure**   See the two words within **pressure**: **press** and sure.

The pressure can **press** on you.

The pressure can **sure** press on you.

Remembering the **press** in pressure helps with the double 's'.

→ **accident**

When two cars collide, they make a dent.

A car crash makes an instant dent.

→ **island**

An <u>island</u> is **land** surrounded by water.

→ **different** and **difficult**   (Spot the vowels too.)

→ **diffe**rent — rent

Let's rent a **diffe**rent film.

Every Friday film night, we rent a different film.

→ Friday's film about a zombie killer cult is **diffi**cult to watch.

→ **purpose** and **suppose**

There's a pose in suppose and purpose.

What do you **suppose** is the **purpose** of his **pose**?

→ **medicine**

There's a medic in medicine.

hard c ("k" sound) — medic, medical, medicate, paramedic

soft c ("s" sound) — medicine

Exercise. Write the missing words in the gaps:

_ _ _ress   pecu_ _ _ _   _ _ _ _ _ _ine

be_ _ _ve   ca_ _ _ _ar   he_ _ _ _

sepa_ _ _ _e po_ _ _ion

ar_ _ _ent   _ _ _iness

h_ _ _ _ and l_ _ _n   _ _ _ _ _ _ure

acci_ _ _ _   sup_ _ _ _

→ Check your spellings:

ad*dress*, peculiar, medicine, believe, calendar, heart,
separate, position, argument, business, hear and learn, pressure, accident, suppose

→ Write a sentence using your favorite words, then draw a picture to go with it.

_____

_____

Write the missing words in the gap:

For example: <u>**Add**</u> an address.

A _____ will give you medicine.   The pressure can _____ on you.

Don't have an argument while chewing _____.   Separate a _____.

He's a peculiar _____.   Don't believe a _____.

I hear with my _____ and learn.   _____ in a comfortable position.

It's good business to go by _____.   Can you _____ me a calendar?

Let's _____ a different movie.   The car has a _____ since the accident.

Use the word-within-word trick or spotting the vowels method to decide which is correct.

1. a. medicine
   b. medisine

2. a. peculier
   b. peculiar

3. a. grammer
   b. grammar

4. a. remember
   b. remembar

5. a. experiance
   b. experience

6. a. accident
   b. accidant

7. a. argument
   b. arguement

8. a. calendar
   b. calandar

9. a. beleive
   b. believe

10. a. business
    b. buisiness

11. a. presure
    b. pressure

12. a. apears
    b. appears

13. a. seperate
    b. separate

14. a. adress
    b. address

15. a. different
    b. differant

Answers

1. a. medicine
   b. medisine

2. a. peculier
   b. peculiar

3. a. grammer
   b. grammar

4. a. remember
   b. remembar

5. a. experiance
   b. experience

6. a. accident
   b. accidant

7. a. argument
   b. arguement

8. a. calendar
   b. calendar

9. a. beleive
   b. believe

10. a. business
    b. buisiness

11. a. presure
    b. pressure

12. a. apears
    b. appears

13. a. seperate
    b. separate

14. a. adress
    b. address

15. a. different
    b. differant

→ Do you need to work on any of these words?

Exercise

Find the word within the word. Underline it. Write it out.

For example: Underline an *animal* in **edu<u>cat</u>ion**: <u>cat</u>

1. Underline something that's *not true* in **believe**: _____

2. Underline a *past tense verb* meaning *end of life* in **studied**: _____

3. Underline a type of *transport* in **business**: _____

4. Underline the *final part* in **friend**: _____

5. Underline *a part of the head* in **learn**: _____

6. Underline a *number* in **money**: _____

7. Underline another word for *everything* in **usually**: _____

8. Underline another word for *hello* in **while**: _____

Answers

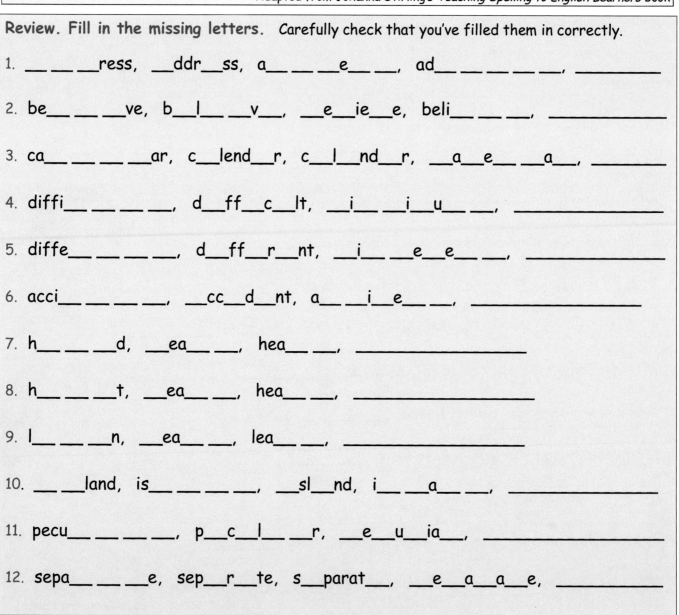

1. Underline something that's *not true* in **bel__ieve**: <u>lie</u>

2. Underline a *past tense verb* meaning *end of life* in **stud__ied**: <u>died</u>

3. Underline a type of *transport* in **b__us__iness**: <u>bus</u>

4. Underline the *final part* in **fri__end**: <u>end</u>

5. Underline *a part of the head* in **l__ear__n**: <u>ear</u>

6. Underline a *number* in **m__one__y**: <u>one</u>

7. Underline another word for *everything* in **us__all__y**: <u>all</u>

8. Underline another word for *hello* in **wh__i__le**: <u>hi</u>

Adapted from Johanna Stirling's *Teaching Spelling to English Learners* book

---

Review. Fill in the missing letters.   Carefully check that you've filled them in correctly.

1. __ __ __ress, __ddr__ss, a__ __ __e__ __, ad__ __ __ __ __, _____

2. be__ __ __ve, b__l__ __v__, __e__ie__e, beli__ __ __, _____

3. ca__ __ __ __ar, c__lend__r, c__l__nd__r, __a__e__ __a__, _____

4. diffi__ __ __ __, d__ff__c__lt, __i__ __i__u__ __, _____

5. diffe__ __ __ __, d__ff__r__nt, __i__ __e__e__ __, _____

6. acci__ __ __ __, __cc__d__nt, a__ __i__e__ __, _____

7. h__ __ __d, __ea__ __, hea__ __, _____

8. h__ __ __t, __ea__ __, hea__ __, _____

9. l__ __ __n, __ea__ __, lea__ __, _____

10. __ __land, is__ __ __ __ __, __sl__nd, i__ __a__ __, _____

11. pecu__ __ __ __, p__c__l__ __r, __e__u__ia__, _____

12. sepa__ __ __e, sep__r__te, s__parat__, __e__a__a__e, _____

Homophone Preparation

In the next section, we're going to look at homophones.

➡ Do you know what **homophones** are? Check these homophones out. What do you notice when you read them out loud?

peace/piece, plain/plane, weight/wait, through/threw, grown/groan, break/brake, herd/heard

➡ Did you notice how they have the same sound but different spellings and meanings?

We're going to look at how using words within words and other memory tricks can help us figure out which homophone to use.

➡ Homophone preparation exercise

➡ Read these and decide which word in bold is correct. Cross out the incorrect ones.

➡ If you don't know or are not sure, then don't worry. We're going to look at how to figure out which word to use later.

1. I'd like a **piece/peace** of that cake, but if I get caught, they'll **grown/groan** at me.

2. It's **plain/plane** to see he really wants a **piece/peace** of that cake.

3. She's listening to music **through/threw** her headphones.

4. The **plain/plane** is landing.

5. I want a **break/brake** from all this homework.

Remembering Which Homophone is Which

Which witch is which?

➜Let's start by getting to know and making friends with some homophones.

➜Read these out loud and notice how they have the same sound but different spellings and meanings:

weight/wait	*which/witch*	*threw/through*
coarse/course	*meat/meet*	*heard/herd*
groan/grown	*plain/plane*	*break/brake*

➜These are **homophones**.

➜ **Homophones** are words with the same sound but different meanings and different spellings.

There are hundreds of homophones in English, and knowing which homophone to use can be tricky.

Sometimes, when we write quickly, we write the first homophone that goes into our brain. That's why it's so important to re-read your work and try to spot these. We're going to look at some memory tricks to help you figure out which homophone is which.

Answers

1. I'd like a **piece** of that cake, but if I get caught, they'll **groan** at me.

2. It's **plain** to see he really wants a **piece** of that cake.

3. She's listening to music **through** her headphones.

4. The **plane** is landing.

5. I want a **break** from all this homework.

➜Please note that if you don't have any problems knowing which word is which, then move on and work on the words that are a problem.

→Seeing words within words and **using a relevant saying** is excellent for remembering which **homophone** is which. Spotting vowels and noticing letter patterns are great too.

Write your memory tricks **and do some** *word art.*

peace / piece
→ peace is ace
→ piece of pie

plain / plane
→ A plain white T-shirt.
→ Land a plane in a lane.

grown / groan
→ I'm all **grown** up and can stay home on my own.
→ To **moan** and **groan** is so annoying.

brake / break
→ He had to brake hard to avoid slamming into the idiot, and his car's brakes screeched.

→You **break** your nightly **fast** at breakfast, so eat a good breakfast.
break bread, a break in the weather

23

hear / here

→ Hear with your **ear** and **lear**n.

→ **H**ere, t**here**, w**here**, every**where**.

---

meet / meat

→ **Meet** me at the next **mee**ting.

→ Take a s**eat** and let's **eat** m**eat**.

Exercise

Fill in the gaps with the correct homophone.

1. (peace/piece)

   She's at _____ with herself while she's in her _____ of heaven — on her boat.

2. (hear/here) Can you _____ that noise coming from right _____?

3. (meat/meet) Do you eat _____? If so, let's _____ at the Beefeater restaurant.

4. (brake/break)
   He slammed his foot on the _____, so he didn't _____ the speed limit.

5. (groan/grown) When I'm a _____-up, I won't moan and _____.

6. (plane/plain) When I'm on a _____, I like to eat _____ food.

Answers

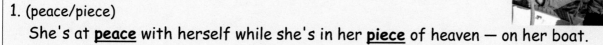

1. (peace/piece)
   She's at **peace** with herself while she's in her **piece** of heaven — on her boat.

2. (hear/here) Can you **hear** that noise coming from right **here**?

3. (meat/meet) Do you eat **meat**? If so let's **meet** at the Beefeater restaurant.

4. (brake/break) He slammed his foot on the **brake**, so he didn't **break** the speed limit.

5. (groan/grown) When I'm a **grown**-up, I won't moan and **groan**.

6. (plane/plain)   When I'm on a **plane**, I like to eat **plain** food.

➔ Write a couple of sentences like these. Draw a picture too.

_____

_____

_____

Let's look at some important words that have some tricky vowel patterns in them:

weight, heard, through, coarse

These are some of the trickiest words to learn. But they're easy to learn with some memory tricks. Before we dive into the tips, do you know what these words mean?

weight, heard, through, coarse

1. Which one is the past tense of *hear?* _____

2. Which one is a measurement of how heavy something or someone is? _____

3. Which one means *not smooth* but *rough?* _____

4. Which one means going from one end to the other? _____

➔ Draw a line to the picture that has something to do with the words:

   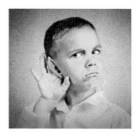

weight, heard, through, coarse

Answers

1. Which one is the past tense of *hear?* <u>heard</u>

2. Which one is a measurement of how heavy something or someone is? <u>weight</u>

3. Which one means *not smooth* but *rough?* <u>coarse</u>

4. Which one means going from one end to the other? <u>through</u>

➔ Do some *word art* for *weight, coarse, heard, through:*

➔ Write a sentence for these words:

_____ (coarse)

(weight)_____

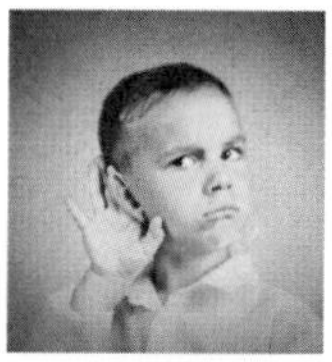

_____(heard)

_____(through)

→ Do you know the homophone partners that go with these words — coarse, weight, heard, through?

→ Read them out loud to help. Have a guess. It's fine if you're wrong or don't know.

→ Here are some picture clues:

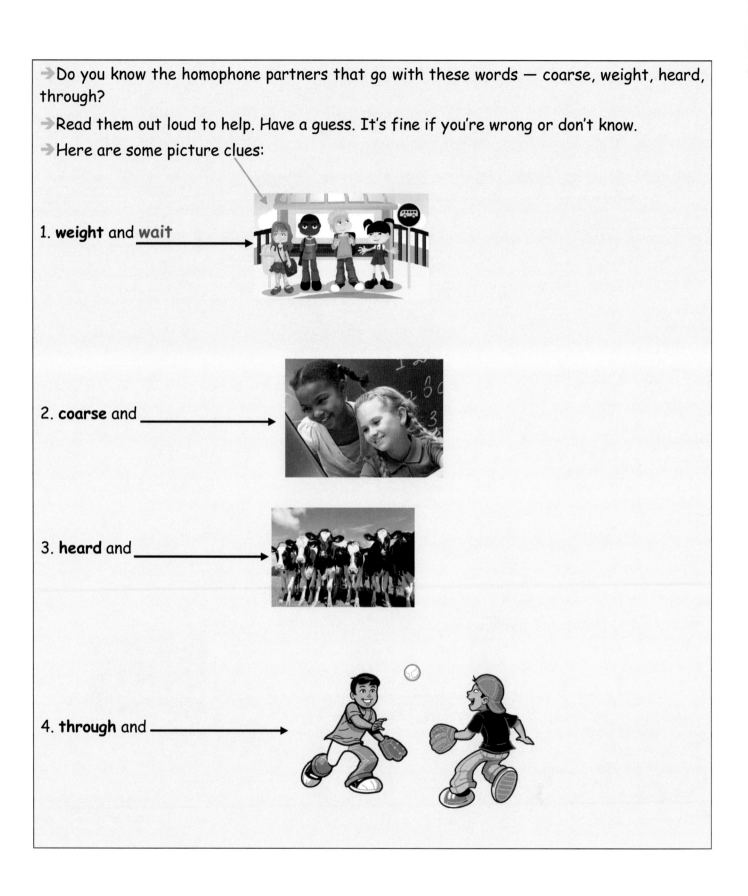

1. **weight** and wait

2. **coarse** and _____

3. **heard** and _____

4. **through** and _____

Answers

→ 1. weight/**wait**   *To **wait** for a bus is so boring.*

→ 2. coarse/**course**   *They took an advanced computer **course**.*

→ 3. heard/**herd**   *A lovely **herd** of cows.*

→ 4. through/**threw**   *He **threw** the ball to his friend.*

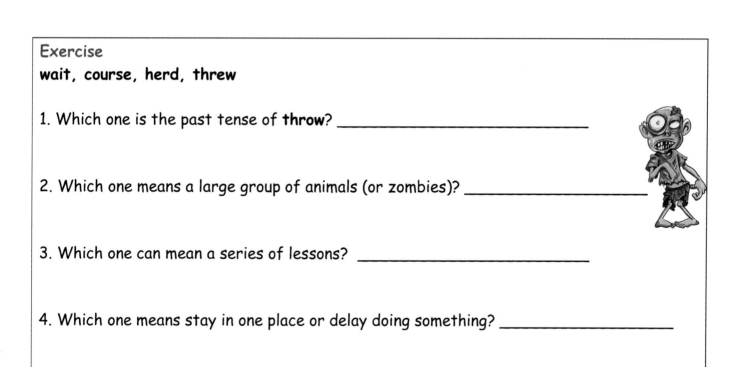

Exercise

wait, course, herd, threw

1. Which one is the past tense of **throw**? _____

2. Which one means a large group of animals (or zombies)? _____

3. Which one can mean a series of lessons? _____

4. Which one means stay in one place or delay doing something? _____

➔**Let's study these words and look at some memory tricks.**

weight/wait

Write your memory tricks **and do some** *word art.*

weight
My **weight** is one hundred and eight.
Weights for **weight**lifting.

wait
Wait for the fish to take the bait.

Fill in the missing letters:

➔ w__ __ght,   wei__ __t,   __ei __ __ __,   _____

➔ w__ __t,   w__ __ __,   __ai__,   _____

➔Write a sentence with both words if you can. *If you can't wait to lose weight, start weightlifting.*

_____

_____

coarse/course

*The grass on the golf **course** was **coarse**.* **Write your** memory, tricks **and do some** *word art.*

---

coarse = rough — not smooth

coarse sand/salt/hair/hands/linen, etc.

The pig has a **coarse coat**.

Keep the "e" when adding ly: ***Coarse**ly chopped vegetables. Coarsely ground pepper.*

coarse

a rough c**oa**rse co**a**t

---

course

a math/physics/computer/art **course**

a golf course, a racecourse, the main course, in due course

Of course

Of course, this is a golf course.

A **u**niversity course.

open **u**p the c**o**urse

Fill in the missing letters:

→ c__ __ rs___, coa__ __ e, __ oa__ ___e, _____

→ c__ __rs__, cou__ __ __, __ou__ __ e, _____

→Write a sentence with both words in it if you can.

_____

_____

heard/herd

*I **heard** about a lovely **herd** of cows.*

Write your memory tricks and do some *word art.*

Heard is the past tense of **hear**.

I heard a strange sound last night.

Hear with your ear. I heard that!

---

herd

a **herd** of elephants, a **herd** of cows, a **herd** of zombies

I'm a nerd and like the herd of zombies on *Walking Dead*.

Fill in the missing letters:

➔ h__ __ __d,   __ea__ __,   __ __ __ __ __d,   __ __ __ __ __ __ __ __ __ __

➔ h__ __d,   h__ __rd,   he__ __,   h __ __ __ __,   __ __ __ __ __ __ __ __

➔ Write a sentence with both words in it if you can.

_____

_____

through/threw

*He **threw** the ball right **through** the hoop.*

Your memory tricks **and** *word art.*

through

*I enjoy walking **through** the park with my parents.*

→ Notice the thr pattern (three, throw, threw, throat).

→ We can use a *verb + through: click through, walk through,* go through, run through, cut through, rush through, look through, think through, etc.

Go around or through the rough grass in the park.

threw

Threw is the past tense of throw.

throw threw

Threw sounds and looks like: drew, crew, chew, few, new, knew, flew, screw, etc.

Fill in the missing letters:

→thr__ __gh, th__ __ __ __ __ __, __ __ __ough, __ __rou__ __, _____

→thr__w, thr__ __, __ __ __ew, _____

→Write a sentence with both words in it if you can.

_____

_____

→ **Proofreading** is a very important skill to develop.

Proofreading your writing means going over your work slowly to spot errors, to see if the sentences sound right, to check there are no missing words and letters, and to see if you've used the right homophones.

Proofreading Exercise

Are the homophones used in these sentences correct or incorrect? Rewrite the homophone errors*. Use your memory tricks.

1. We went **threw** the park on our way home.

2. I hope you didn't **wait** too long.

3. My sister is taking a pre-med **course**.

4. I **herd** the news this morning and it was depressing.

5. I **through** the ball hard.

6. I go **through** the park on my way to school.

Clue: There are three sentences that have the correct homophone.

---

*You're only just learning these words so don't be hard on yourself if you can't decide which is right or not.

Learning anything takes a few goes and a bit of brainpower so go over the previous pages again.

Answers

through
1. We went ~~threw~~ the park on our way home.

2. I hope you didn't **wait** too long. ✓

3. My sister is taking a pre-med **course**. ✓

heard
4. I ~~herd~~ the news this morning and it was depressing.

threw
5. I ~~through~~ the ball hard.

6. I go **through** the park on my way to school. ✓

Do you need to revise any of these words?

→ Prefixes, root words and suffixes preparation

In the next section, we're looking at **prefixes, root words,** and **suffixes.** Knowing these and noticing them will help you spell and read long words.

Do you know what **prefixes, root words,** and **suffixes** are?

Look at these words and see how they are built with a prefix, **root word,** and suffix. Add these words to the diagram below.   (Answers on the next page.)

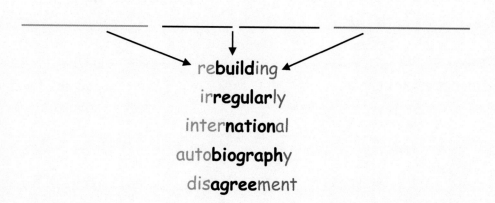

Building Words with Root Words, Prefixes, and Suffixes

Never be scared of long words ever again — read on.

➜ Let's start getting to know and making friends with prefixes and suffixes. These are fantastic friends to have because they can help us spell and read long words instead of getting scared of them.

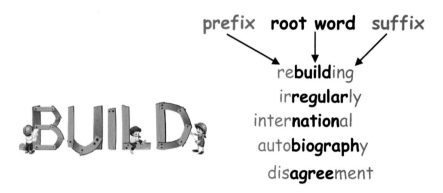

prefix **root word** suffix

re**build**ing
ir**regular**ly
inter**nation**al
auto**biograph**y
dis**agree**ment

We add prefixes and suffixes to **root words** (complete words).

Prefixes are little words we add to the beginning of root words to make the word negative or to add extra information.

We're going to look at some prefixes that are important to learn: **un, dis, re, in, mis, super, anti, auto, im, il.**

disagree, unhealthy, unlucky, superman/Superman, superpower
immature, impossible, insane, incorrect
autopilot, illegal

We add prefixes to the beginning of root words, usually without any changes in spelling.

There are hundreds of prefixes. Some of the most popular are: **in-, un-, dis-, mis-, ir-, il-, im-, pre-, ex-, anti-, uni-**

➜ Some common prefixes are un-, re-, in-, dis-, mis-. Write a couple of words with these.

Prefixes

un-, re-, in-, dis-, mis- **prefixes**

➔ **un-** (not) ➔ **un** + happy = **unhappy** = **not** happy
unusual, uncomfortable, unbelievable, unnatural, unsure, uncertain, unfriendly, unknown, uneasy, unhealthy, unsteady, unfair, unlucky, unpopular

➔ **re-** (do something again, repeat, return, go back) ➔ **re** + paint = **repaint** = paint (it) again
redo, retry, rebuild, replay, reappear, redecorate, refresh, reuse, recycle, rewrite, react, return

➔ **in-** (not) ➔ **in** + correct = **incorrect** = not correct = wrong = not right
incomplete, inactive, insane, indestructible, inexperienced

➔ **dis-** (to make opposite, negative) ➔ **dis** + appear = **disappear** = not be seen
disagree, disobey, disappoint, dishonest, dissatisfied, discontinued

➔ **mis-** (done wrong/badly) ➔ **mis** + behave = **misbehave** = behave badly
mislead, misspell, mismanage, misguide, misdirect, misplace

Exercise

Write the meanings of these words:

For example, *unsure* = <u>not sure</u>, *redo* = <u>do it again</u>, *incorrect* = not correct

1. unhealthy = _____

2. rewrite = _____

3. incomplete = _____

4. unpopular = _____

5. ungrateful = _____

6. redo = _____

7. unfair = _____

8. uncomfortable = _____

9. reuse = _____

10. inactive = _____

Answers

1. unhealthy = <u>not healthy</u>
2. rewrite = <u>write it again</u>
3. incomplete = <u>not complete</u>
4. unpopular = <u>not popular.</u>
5. ungrateful = <u>not grateful</u>
6. redo = <u>do it again</u>
7. unfair = <u>not fair</u>
8. uncomfortable = <u>not comfortable</u>
9. reuse = <u>use it again</u>
10. inactive = <u>not active</u>

→ Notice the double letters in the following words. We add a prefix to the root word which creates double letters: ◄────────────────────

dis + satisfied = di<u>ss</u>atisfied

mis + spell = mi<u>ss</u>pell

im + mature = i<u>mm</u>ature

il + legal = i<u>ll</u>egal

ir + responsible = i<u>rr</u>esponsible

ir + regular = i<u>rr</u>egular

un + natural = u<u>nn</u>atural

→ **Remember to use a dictionary if you don't understand a word.**

Some prefixes have opposites:

in / ex	in / de	im / ex
include / **ex**clude	**in**flate / **de**flate	**im**port / **ex**port
inhale / **ex**hale	increase / decrease	implode / explode

Prefix rules

→ Can you see the prefix rules in these words?

> → illegal, illegible
>
> → irregular, irresponsible
>
> → immature, immortal
>
> → impossible, impatient

*He's an **immortal** and so **impatient**, but thank goodness he's not **immature** or **irresponsible**.*

Prefix Rules and Exceptions

There are plenty of exceptions to these rules, but pronunciation can help.

Use **il** before words starting with **l**:

legal — **il**legal   *That's not legal - that's illegal.*

legible — **il**legible   *I can't read this — it's illegible.*

logical — illogical   *That's stupid and doesn't make sense — it's totally illogical.*

(But also consider *unlawful, unless* — the "un" helps the pronunciation.)

Use **ir** before words starting with **r**:

relevant — **ir**relevant   *That question is irrelevant.*

regular — **ir**regular   *She works different shifts and her hours are irregular.*

responsible — irresponsible   *Their behavior was so irresponsible.*

(But also consider *unreal, unrated* — the "un" helps the pronunciation.)

Use **im** before words starting with **m** and **p**:

mature — **im**mature   *My dad's so immature — I'm the mature one!*

mortal — **im**mortal   *Vampires are immortal and live forever until staked!*

possible — impossible   *Everything is possible even though you think it's impossible.*

perfect — **im**perfect   *We're living in an imperfect world.*

patient — impatient   *He gets impatient with people who don't agree with him.*

(But also consider *unmarked, unmarried, unpack, unpick, unpaid*
— the "un" helps the pronunciation.)

→ **Remember to use a dictionary if you don't understand a word.**

Exercises

Add a prefix to these words:

For example: **not regular** = <u>irregular</u>

not possible = _____   not perfect = _____

not patient = _____   not mature = _____

not relevant = _____   not legal = _____

not logical = _____   not regular = _____

Check your spellings in the lists on the previous page.

→ Choose two favorite words and do some *word art*.

→ Write a sentence with these words, and draw a picture.

_____

_____

Prefix Exercise 1

Make these into the opposite meaning by adding a prefix.

For example: legal — <u>illegal</u>

1. certain — _____

2. honest — _____

3. real — _____

4. popular — _____

5. mature — _____

6. happy — _____

7. complete — _____

8. responsible — _____

9. possible — _____

10. correct — _____

Prefix Exercise 2

Add **un-**, **re-**, **in-** or **dis-** to these words to make the opposite meaning.

1. __cycle   2. ___certain   3. ___natural   4. ____agree   5. ___correct

6. ___sure   7. ___fair   8. ___honest   9. ____complete   10. ___appear

Exercise 1 Answers

1. certain — <u>uncertain</u>
2. honest — <u>dishonest</u>
3. real — <u>unreal</u>
4. popular — <u>unpopular</u>
5. mature — <u>immature</u>
6. happy — <u>unhappy</u>
7. complete — <u>incomplete</u>
8. responsible — <u>irresponsible</u>
9. possible — <u>impossible</u>
10. correct — <u>incorrect</u>

Exercise 2 Answers

1. **re**turn   2. **un**certain   3. **un**natural   4. **dis**agree   5. **in**correct

6. **un**sure   7. **un**fair   8. **dis**honest   9. **in**complete   10. **dis**appear

➜ What do you think these prefixes mean? Have a guess.

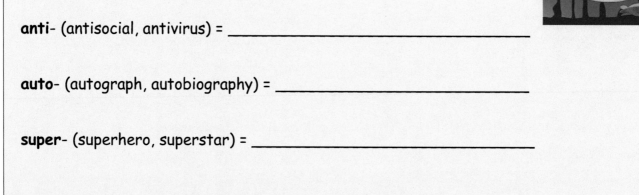

sub- (submarine, submerge, subway) = _____

anti- (antisocial, antivirus) = _____

auto- (autograph, autobiography) = _____

super- (superhero, superstar) = _____

 It's perfectly OK if you don't know. We're going to look at these next.

Common prefixes

sub- means "under" or "close to"
submarine, submerge, subway, subdivide, subheading, subzero

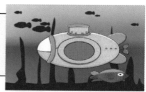

anti- means "against"
antiseptic, antisocial, antimatter, antivirus

auto- means "by yourself/itself"
autobiography, autograph, autopilot, automatic

super- means "above", "beyond", "very big"
supermarket, superstore, superhero, superhuman, superman,
superstar, supermodel, supercool, superpower, supersonic

inter- means "between" or "among"
interact, intercity, international, interface, interstate
intergalactic (between two galaxies)

Rewrite and add the correct prefix (anti, sub, super, auto, inter) to these words:

power — <u>superpower</u>

1. sonic — _____

2. biography — _____

3. merge — _____

4. hero — _____

5. state — _____

6. virus — _____

Answers

1. sonic — <u>supersonic</u>
2. biography — <u>autobiography</u>
3. merge — <u>submerge</u>
4. hero — <u>superhero</u>
5. state — <u>interstate</u>
6. virus — <u>antivirus</u>

Suffixes

Don't forget your **suffixes** and **spelling rules**. A suffix is added to the end of a word to turn it into another word. Suffixes make words even longer.

➔Sometimes we can add a **suffix** to a **root word** without changing anything:

usual — usually — unusually

fresh — refreshed — refreshes

build — builder — building — rebuilds — rebuilding

nation — nations — national — nationality — international

appear — appears — appearing — disappears — disappearance

act — acts — acting — acted — active — action — reacts — reacting — reacted — reaction

➔**Drop the "e" rule** (more on this rule in the next chapter):

behave — behaving — misbehaving

nature — natural — unnatural

believe — believable — unbelievable

adventure — adventurous — unadventurous

arrange — arranging — arranged — rearranged

continue — continued — continuing — continual

➔ Do you know which is correct and **why**? Have a guess (see page 46).
a. writing   b. writeing
a. excitment   b. excitement
a. famous   b. fameous
a. lovly   b. lovely

➔**Doubling up rule with** vowels suffixes (more on this rule later):

stop — stopped — stopping — stopper — stoppable — stoppage — unstoppable

forget — forgetting — unforgettable

forgot — forgotten

quiz — quizzes — quizzing — quizzed

➔**"y" to "i" rule** if the root word has more than one syllable:

beauty — beautiful, penny — penniless

happy — happily — unhappily — happiness — unhappiness

Rewrite and use different colors to separate the **root word**, prefix, and **suffix**.

disagreement ➜ dis<u>agree</u>ment = dis + agree + ment

Remember, we drop the "e" in some root words:

undecided ➜ un<u>decide</u>d = un + decide + ed

	Write the root word here.
	<u>agree</u>
	<u>decide</u>
rebuilding _____	_____
unhelpful _____	_____
discontinued _____	_____
irregularly _____	_____
disappearance _____	_____
international _____	_____
unfriendly _____	_____
incompletely _____	_____
unbelievable _____	_____
unnoticed _____	_____
disrespectful _____	_____

Answers	root words
rebuilding — rebuilding = re + **build** + ing ⟶	build
unhelpful — unhelpful = un + **help** + ful	help
discontinued — discontinued = dis + **continue** + ed	continue
irregularly — irregularly = ir + **regular** + ly	regular
disappearance — disappearance = dis + **appear** + ance	appear
international — international = inter + **nation** + al	nation
unfriendly — unfriendly = un + **friend** + ly	friend
incompletely — incompletely = in + **complete** + ly	complete
unbelievable — unbelievable = un + **believe** + able	believe
unnoticed — unnoticed = un + **notice** + ed	notice
disrespectful — disrespectful = dis + **respect** + ful	respect

Spelling rules

Drop the "e"

Answers: a. writing   b. excitement   a. famous   b. lovely

→ Notice the vowel and consonant suffixes:

drop the e	keep the e
write → writing	love → lovely
fame → famous	excite → excitement

→ Drop the "e" when adding a vowel suffix ending: **-ing, -ous, -ed, -er, -est, -ize, -able**

*write + **ing** = writing*   *arrive — arrival, arriving, arrived*

*fame + **ous** = famous*   *believe — believing, believer, believable, unbelievable*

Exception: We keep the "e" when we add -able to words ending in "g" or "c" to keep the soft "g" and "c" sounds: *manage — manageable, change — changeable, notice — noticeable*

→**Y** is sometimes a vowel. When we add "y" to the end of words, it becomes a vowel suffix and we drop the **e**:

ease + y = *easy*,   laze + y = *lazy*,   shake + y = *shaky*,   slime + y = *slimy*

→Keep the "e" when adding a consonant suffix ending: **-ly, -ment, -s, -ful, -less, -ness**… (with some exceptions we'll see below).

excite + **ment** = *excitement* (keep the "e")   love + **ly** = *lovely* (keep the "e")

lively, writes, hopeful, hopeless, tasteless, blueness

The drop the "e" rule is a great little rule to know, but be warned: like all English spelling rules, there are exceptions.

> **Exceptions**
>
> ➔ For words ending in -**ue**, we drop the "e" with –ly:
> true — truly,　due — duly
>
> According to the Oxford English Dictionary, **truly** is one of the most misspelled words —
> true + ly = truly (drop the "e")
> It's truly hot in July.
>
> ➔ We drop the "e" in argument — argue + ment = **argument**
> See the "gum" in ar**gum**ent — Don't chew **gum** in an ar**gum**ent.

Rules and patterns with **drop the "e" with** -ing:

make — making	write — writing
shake — shaking	bite — biting
bake — baking	excite — exciting
quake — quaking	complete — completing
have — having	delete — deleting
love — loving	concentrate — concentrating
give — giving	fascinate — fascinating
forgive — forgiving	use — using
move — moving	amuse — amusing
improve — improving	excuse — excusing
receive — receiving	come — coming
achieve — achieving	become — becoming
solve — solving	blame — blaming
believe — believing	frame — framing
notice — noticing	create — creating
sneeze — sneezing	describe — describing
manage — managing	shine — shining
cope — coping	bore — boring
escape - escaping	snore — snoring

Keep the "e" with
be — being, eye — eyeing, see — seeing, agree — agreeing, flee — fleeing,
knee — kneeing, referee — refereeing, guarantee — guaranteeing

➔Drop the "e" rule exercise

Rewrite these and add some vowel suffixes (-ing,-al,-ed, -ation, -ion).

For example: arrive — <u>arriving, arrival</u>

believe — _____

circle — _____

complete — _____

guide — _____

decide — _____

describe — _____

imagine — _____

exercise — _____

argue — _____

improve — _____

breathe — _____

continue — _____

fame — _____

increase — _____

promise — _____

separate — _____

Answers on page 50.

Drop or Keep the "e" Exercise

Rewrite the words with the suffixes. Don't forget the rules!

1. care + ing = _____

2. use + ful = _____

3. close + ed = _____

4. shade + y = _____

5. shake + ing = _____

6. argue + ment = _____

7. safe + ty = _____

8. excite + ment = _____

9. amuse + ing = _____

10. true + ly = _____

Answers on page 51.

Some possible answers

arrive — arriving, arrival

believe — believing, believed, believable, unbelievable

circle — circling, circled

complete — completing, completed, completion

guide — guiding, guided

decide — deciding, decided, undecided

describe — describing, described

imagine — imagining, imagined, imagination

exercise — exercising, exercised

argue — arguing, argued, (argument — a common exception)

improve — improving, improved

breathe — breathing, breathed

continue — continuing, continued, continuation, continual

fame — famed, famous

increase — increased, increasing

promise — promising, promised

separate — separating, separated

→ Write a sentence with your favorite word. → Then draw a picture.

_____

_____

Answers

Check your spelling carefully. What are the rules?

1. care + ing = **caring** (drop the "e")

2. use + ful = **useful** (keep the "e")

3. close + ed = **closed**

4. shade + y = **shady**

5. shake + ing = **shaking**

6. argue + ment = **argument** (drop the "e" exception)

7. safe + ty = **safety**

8. excite + ment = **excitement**

9. amuse + ing = **amusing**

10. true + ly = **truly**

How did you do?

➔ Go over the answers and figure out why we spell a word the way that we do.

➔ Go over the rule, exceptions, and patterns again tomorrow.

➔ -tion, -sion, -cian preparation

mention, position, question, occasion, possession, electrician

➔ Why do we spell these "shun" sound endings like this when one spelling would do?

-tion, -sion, -cian

After his sensational television show, everyone wanted to question the magician about his new magical invention.

➔   Underline all the -**tion**, -**sion**, -**cian** words.

➔These "shun" (-tion, -sion, -cian) suffix endings turn verbs into **nouns.**

➔They sound the same, or slightly similar, which can cause problems spelling them.

➔-**tion** is the most common ending.

➔Answers

The History Bit

We have these endings because most of them come from Latin. If the original Latin word ended in -t, -s or -c, then it was used in the English "shun" word.

question from Latin *quaestio(n-)*

pension from Latin *pensio(n-)*

discussion from Latin *discussio(n-)*

magician from Latin *magica*

The people who wrote the first dictionaries didn't care whether we could spell words easily, they just cared about the Latin origins of the word.

➔We have some rules to help us figure out which ending to use — some are easy to spot.

➔Look at these. Can you see the rules?

inven**t** — inven**tion**

direc**t** — direc**tion**

comple**te** — comple**tion**

posses**s** — posses**sion**

revi**se** — revi**sion**

expan**d** — expan**sion**, deci**de** — deci**sion**

permi**t** — permi**ssion**

electri**c** — electri**cian**

Read on to find out if you're right.   It's perfectly OK if you don't know.

-tion

*This is my **suggestion** for the **location** of our next **vacation**.*

1. When words end in t, add ion (-tion):

quest — question	*invent — invention*	*interrupt — interruption*
suggest — suggestion	*prevent — prevention*	*erupt — eruption*
insert — insertion	*digest — digestion*	*exhibit — exhibition*

2. When words end in ct, add ion (-ction):

act — action	*reject — rejection*	*protect — protection*
react — reaction	*inject — injection*	*direct — direction*
collect — collection	*inspect — inspection*	*correct — correction*
select — selection	*product — production*	*subtract — subtraction*
elect — election	*instruct — instruction*	*contract — contraction*
extinct — extinction		

Also, *fiction, fraction*

3. When words end in te, **drop the "e"** and add ion (-tion):

opposite — opposition	*complete — completion*
devote — devotion	*pollute — pollution*
hibernate — hibernation	*emote — emotion*

-tion words without a rule: *mention, condition, attention, solution, caution*

-ation

Adding -**ation** to a verb changes it into a noun.

1. Add ation to make the pronunciation easier:

present — present*ation*	confront — confront*ation*
consult — consult*ation*	tempt — tempt*ation*
inform — inform*ation*	consider — consider*ation*

2. -ate ➜ -ation.
    Change -ate to -ation:

educate — educ*ation*	congratulate — congratul*ations*	separate — separ*ation*
locate — loc*ation*	populate — popul*ation*	hesitate — hesitation
inflate — inflation	relate — relation	decorate — decoration
frustrate — frustration	create — creation	generate — generation
operate — operation	calculate — calculation	

3. Drop the "e" and add ation in these words (-ation):

    invite — invit*ation*   prepare — prepar*ation*

    The "a" makes these -tion words easier to say.
    (You can hear the "a" sound in -**ation**, which helps with spelling them.)

inspire — inspir*ation*	sense — sensation	imagine — imagination
examine — examination	explore — exploration	combine — combin*ation*
adore — adoration	admire — admiration	continue — continuation

4. Change the "y" to "i" and add cation (-ication):

    apply — appl*ication*   qualify — qualification

    multiply — multiplication   identify — identification

5. **Change the "y" to "i" and add** ation (-iation): vary — vari*ation*

54

-ition

Drop the "e" and add ition in these words:

pose — position   compete — competition   define — definition

The "i" makes these -ition words easier to say. You can hear the /I/ sound in -**ition**, which helps with spelling them.

Exercises (Use your knowledge of the rules and pronunciation to help.)

1. **Change these into their -tion nouns:**

act — <u>action</u>   invent — _____

inject — _____   pose — _____

complete — _____   vacate — _____

quest — _____   inform — _____

apply — _____   direct — _____

2. **Write the root word of each word:**

protection — <u>protect</u>   separation — _____

exploration — _____   vacation — _____

qualification — _____   suggestion — _____

location — _____   education — _____

→ Write a sentence about a *vacation*, *location*, or your *education*.

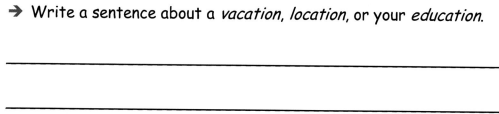

_____

_____

_____

55

Answers

1. Change these into their -tion nouns:

act — action   invent — invention

inject — injection   pose — position

complete — completion   vacate — vacation

quest — question   inform — information

apply — application   direct — direction

2. Write the root word of each word:

protection — protect   separation — separate

exploration — explore   vacation — vacate

qualification — qualify   suggestion — suggest

location — locate   education — educate

➔ **-sion preparation exercise**

➔Can you see how we form the -**sion** from the root word?

discuss — discussion, possess — possession

revise — revision, televise — television

decide — decision, explode — explosion

expand — expansion, extend — extension

permit — permission, admit — admission

-sion

Not as many nouns end in -**sion**.

1. We often form -**sion** **nouns** from verbs ending in -**d**, -**de**, -**se**.

➔ Drop the **de** or **d** and add **sion**:

invade — invasion	*divide — division*	*suspend — suspension*
decide — decision	*explode — explosion*	*expand — expansion*
erode — erosion	*collide — collision*	*comprehend — comprehension*
conclude — conclusion	*intrude — intrusion*	*extend — extension*

Exceptions: *attend — attention, intend — intention*

➔ For words ending in **se**, drop the "e" and add **ion** (-**sion**):

revise — revision	*tense — tension*	*confuse — confusion*
televise — television	*verse — version*	*fuse — fusion*

Also: occasion, pension, mansion

-**ssion**

2. When words end in **ss** just add **ion** (-**ssion**):

discuss — discussion	*confess — confession*	*obsess — obsession*
profess — profession	*possess — possession*	*express — expression*
depress — depression	*process — procession*	

Also: mission, passion, session, aggression

3. -**mit** to -**ssion**

Change **mit** to **mission**: *admit — admission*

permit — permission	*omit — omission*	*commit — commission*
submit — submission	*transmit — transmission*	

➔ You might not remember these rules but hopefully you'll recognize the patterns.

Exercise

Add -**sion** to these words. Can you remember the rules?

explode — _____

divide — _____

possess — _____

expand — _____   collide — _____

revise — _____   conclude — _____

discuss — _____   admit — _____

permit — _____   invade — _____

extend — _____

Check your spellings against the lists of words on the previous page.

-cian

-**cian** endings usually mean occupation, profession, or job: *electrician, politician, magician*

Some of these are made out of words ending in -**c**, so we just add ian (-**cian**):

    music — musician   *magic — magician*

    electric — electrician   *optic — optician*

    politic — politician   *mathematic — mathematician*

Also: beauty — beautician

Exercise

1. Someone who works with electricity is an _____.

2. *Dynamo* is a famous _____ who does amazing magic tricks.

6. They play musical instruments and are often in bands or orchestras — they're

_____.

7. She loves math and wants to be a _____.

8. Someone who is active in government usually as an elected official:

_____.

-tion, -sion, -cian summary

➔ Look at these. Can you remember the rules?

    invent — invention, suggest — suggestion, invent — invention, opt — option

    act — action, inject — injection, direct — direction, product — production

    present — presentation, confront — confrontation, expect — expectation

    complete — completion, devote — devotion, pollute — pollution, hibernate — hibernation

    educate — education, hesitate — hesitation, create — creation

    invite — invitation, inspire — inspiration, prepare — preparation

    compete — competition, pose — position, define — definition

    discuss — discussion, possess — possession

    revise — revision, televise — television

    decide — decision, explode — explosion

    expand — expansion, extend — extension

    permit — permission, admit — admission

    electric — electrician, magic — magician, music — musician

Answers

1. Someone who works with electricity is an **electrician**.

2. Dynamo is a famous **magician** who does amazing magic tricks.

6. They play musical instruments and are often in bands or orchestras — they're **musicians**.

7. She loves math and wants to be a **mathematician**.

8. Someone who is active in government usually as an elected official: **politician**.

Word search

Words can go forwards, backwards, diagonally, vertically, horizontally!

This one is tricky — can you do it? I bet you can, but it's going to make you go ➡

completion
conclusion
discussion
electrician
explosion
information
magician
mention
occasion
position
possession
question

```
b r q h n f t k j j e o o n e
g y u n m n x i u l p f c a n
h m e l o z d t e n n r d i o
s b s v p i t c y s p u u c i
n p t n o i t a m r o f n i s
c f i j u r n e p p n t w g s
e x o v i o e o l o r s n a e
j e n c i b s x i p f h r m s
d v i t l i q s p d m c t l s
z a n c t n s a q l j o i z o
n e y i x u o b r y o v c n p
m c o n c l u s i o n s v e f
c n a s n o i s a c c o i i b
a h i s q j e h l s z s q o t
g d b n p m h n a g f i z j n
```

60

➜ **Adding -ly preparation**

Next, we're going to look at adding the suffix -ly to words.

Which is correct?				
1. a. probably	2. a. actualy	3. a. lovly	4. a. accidentaly	5. a. happyly
b. probablely	b. actually	b. lovely	b. accidentally	b. happily

➜ Can you see the rules? Have a guess.

What about words ending in l?	What about these words?	What do we do with the e?
⬇	⬇	⬇
natural + ly = naturally	certain + ly = certainly	complete + ly = completely
special + ly = specially	different + ly = differently	extreme + ly = extremely
cool + ly = coolly	important + ly = importantly	possible + ly = possibly
careful + ly = carefully	regular + ly = regularly	What about this e?
		possible ➜ possibly
		gentle ➜ gently

These are explained in Rules 1 + 2   Rule 3   Rules 4 + 5

 It's perfectly OK if you don't know. We're going to discover the rules next.

Answers: 1. a. probably (rule 5)   2. b. actually (rule 1)   3. b. lovely (rule 4)
4. b. accidentally (rule 1)   5. b. happily (rule 6)

Adding -ly to Words

I **occasionally** read a book, but I **probably** should read more because
I **actually** enjoy reading.

Rule 1: *Actually, this **really** is a **totally** easy rule.*

Add ly to words ending in "l" (-lly):

cool + ly = coolly

real + ly = really

woolly

faithfully

Notice these -ally patterns:

usual + ly = usually

actual + ly = actually

real + ly = really

final + ly = finally

total — totally

social — socially

accidental — accidentally

occasional — occasionally

Rule 2: *Carefully does it, and **hopefully** you'll understand.*

Adding ly to words ending in -**ful** makes -fully (notice the double "l"):

careful + ly = carefully

beautiful + ly = beautifully

successful — successfully

playful — playfully

hopeful — hopefully

thoughtful — thoughtfully

*That was **beautifully** done! Now that you've **successfully** read this, go to the next page.*

Rule 3: *I hope this is going* **smoothly** *so far.*

Add ly to most words (-ly):

slow + ly = slowly

stupid — stupidly

sad — sadly

quick — quickly

quiet — quietly

loud — loudly

part — partly

short — shortly

proud — proudly

smooth — smoothly

kind / unkind — kindly / unkindly

friend — friendly, unfriendly

If you need to go **slowly**, *that's fine.*

Rule 4: *It's* **lovely** *to feel* **completely** *happy.*

Keep the **e** (-ely):

lone + ly = lonely

love + ly = lovely

live + ly = lively

like + ly = likely

brave — bravely

close — closely

nice — nicely

safe — safely

sure — surely

complete — completely

extreme — extremely

separate — separately

Exceptions: Drop the **e** in:

true + ly = ***truly*** ⟸ **Truly** is one of the most misspelled words in English.

due + ly = duly

whole + ly = wholly

It's truly hot in July.

63

Rule 5: *This **probably** looks **incredibly** hard.*
Change the **e** to y in words ending in a consonant + **le (-ly)**: probable — probably

gentle — gently	possible — possibly	terrible — terribly
simple — simply	responsible — responsibly	horrible — horribly
incredible — incredibly	humble — humbly	sensible — sensibly

Rule 6: *Luckily, this is nearly the end.*
For two-syllable words ending in **consonant + y**, change the y to i (-ily):

easy — easily, uneasily
angry — angrily
happy — happily, unhappily
busy — busily
crazy — crazily
lazy — lazily
ready — readily
hungry — hungrily
ordinary — ordinarily
noisy — noisily
lucky — luckily, unluckily

But we keep the "y" in one-syllable words:

shy + ly = shyly
sly + ly = slyly
dry + ly = dryly or drily

Rule 7: We add **-ally** to words ending in -ic (**-cally**):

basic + ally = *basically* comic + ally = *comically*

cynically, ethically, logically, magically, medically, musically

A big exception is *publicly = public + ly*

If a word ends in **-al** just add **-ly (-ally)**:

accidental → accidentally	occasional → occasionally	original → originally
incidental → incidentally	musical → musically	experimental → experimentally

Notice how these words are built:

act → actual → actually

magic → magical → magically

music → musical → musically

drama → dramatic → dramatical → dramatically

occasion → occasional → occasionally

accident → accidental → accidentally

experiment → experimental → experimentally

continue → (drop the "e") → continual → continually

nature → (drop the "e" and add "al") → natural → naturally

probable → (drop the "e" and add "y") → probably

Fill in the missing letters:

a__ __i__e__ __a__ __ __, acci__ __ __ __ __ally, __cc__d__nt__lly,

_____

o__ __a__io__a__ __ __ __, occa__ __ __ __ __ally, __cc__s__ __n__lly,

_____

__ctu__lly, a__ __ua__ __ __ __, __ct__ __lly, __ __ __ually,

_____

pr__b__bly, proba__ __ __, __ __o__a__ __ __, pro__ __ __ly,

_____

m__g__c__lly, magic__ __ __ __, __a__i__a__ __ __,

_____

Exercise

Rewrite these and add **ly**.

Remember the rules for these — check on the previous pages, or opposite, if you can't.
For example, certain = <u>certainly</u>

1. love — _____

2. hopeful — _____

3. final — _____

4. complete — _____

5. extreme — _____

6. important — _____

7. particular — _____

8. happy — _____

9. quarter — _____

10. special — _____

11. occasional — _____

12. probable — _____

13. possible — _____

14. basic — _____

15. gentle — _____

16. different — _____

17. natural — _____

18. recent — _____

19. regular — _____

20. separate — _____

21. strange — _____

22. natural — _____

23. actual — _____

24. true — _____

Answers on page 68.

7 rules around adding ly — the quick version

1. Add ly to other words ending in "l" (-lly):

   real + ly = really   actual + ly = actually   accidental — accidentally
   cool + ly = coolly   usual + ly = usually   occasional — occasionally

2. Add ly to words ending in -**ful** to make –fully:

   careful + ly = carefully   hope + ful + ly = hopefully
   use + ful + ly = usefully   thought + ful + ly = thoughtfully

3. Add -**ly** to whole words (-ly):

   slow + ly = slowly   friend — friendly
   quick — quickly   certain — certainly

4. Keep the "e" (-**ely**):

   lone — lonely   strange — strangely
   love — lovely   complete — completely

   Exception: Drop the "e" in *true — truly (It's truly hot in July.)*

5. Change the end **e** to **y** in words ending in a **consonant** + le (-bly, -ply, -tly):

   gentle — gently   simple — simply
   possible — possibly   probable — probably

6. For two-syllable words ending in a **consonant** + y, change the y to i (-ily):

   happy — happily   busy — busily
   angry — angrily   crazy — crazily

7. Add –**ally** to words ending in -**ic** (-ically):

   basic + ally = *basically*,   comic + ally = *comically*

   An exception is *publicly = public + ly*

   If a word ends in -**al**, just add -**ly**: accidental ➜ accidentally, occasional ➜ occasionally

Answers

Check your spelling carefully.

In words ending in e, did you keep or change it, or drop it for one key word*?

1. love — **lovely**

2. hopeful — **hopefully**

3. final — **finally**

4. complete — **completely**

5. extreme — **extremely**

6. important — **importantly**

7. particular — **particularly**

8. happy — **happily**

9. quarter — **quarterly**

10. special — **specially**

11. occasional — **occasionally**

12. probable — **probably**

13. possible — **possibly**

14. basic — **basically**

15. gentle — **gently**

16. different — **differently**

17. natural — **naturally**

18. recent — **recently**

19. regular — **regularly**

20. separate — **separately**

21. strange — **strangely**

22. natural — **naturally**

23. actual — **actually**

*24. true — **truly** (drop the "e")
   truly is often misspelled

➔How did you do? Do you need to go over some of these rules or words again?

-ly Word Search

Words can go forwards, backwards, diagonally, vertically, horizontally!

accidentally
actually
basically
carefully
coolly
hopefully
lovely
luckily
naturally
occasionally
particularly
peculiarly
possibly
probably
really
regularly
truly
usually

```
y y c m w y v c v l i h y w r
l l r e a l l y o v o l c c e
l l a y u p j v r o l u a o g
a a d e l s e l v a l r p y u
t r l o s l j c n v e l l m l
n u z v y g a o u f y l y b a
e t p a r t i c u l a r l y r
d a w n j s l l i u i t y y l
i n l a a p l k t s y a c y y
c j y c a y c c n f a e r l d
c z c r r u a k e i b b g l x
a o y l l u f e p o h t k a y
u u t p r o b a b l y q n u l
y l b i s s o p y l u r t s k
h f s u l x k o x n x f q u j
```

➜ **-ous preparation exercise**

Which is correct?

1. a. various
   b. varyous

2. a. famous
   b. fameous

3. a. marvalous
   b. marvelous

4. a. glamorous
   b. glamourous

-ous

We have *various, marvelous, adventurous* words in this section.

→ We add -**ous** to nouns to make adjectives (describing words).

→ These -**ous** adjectives add more meaning than using *great, bad, good nice, lovely.*

→ -**ous** is from Latin and means *full of, having to do with, all about, a quality:* *glorious* = full of glory, *joyous* = full of joy, *courageous* = full of courage.

Answers: 1. a. various   2. a. famous   3. b. marvelous   4. a. glamorous

---

Spelling Rules:

1. **Add** ous **to root words** (complete words): *dangerous, poisonous, mountainous, joyous,* humorous, marvelous

Sometimes, there's no obvious root word: *tremendous, enormous, jealous, serious, obvious, curious, previous*

2. **Change the end "y" to "i" when adding** ous (-ious): *vary — various*
   (You can hear the i/"ee" sound when you say these.)
   glory — glorious,   fury — furious,   mystery — mysterious

3. **Drop the "e" when adding** ous: *fame — famous*
   nerve — nervous,   adventure — adventurous,   continue — continuous

4. **But keep the "e" with these** -ous **words:** (You can hear the "e" when you say these.)
   hideous, courteous, spontaneous

5. **Keep the "e" in these words to keep the soft "g" sound** (-geous):
   outrage — outrageous,   courage — courageous,   gorgeous

6. **Add –ly to make adverbs** (-ously):
   previously, seriously, nervously, cautiously, viciously, spontaneously, graciously

7. glamour
   Drop the "u" in glamour when adding ous (-orous): *glamour — glamorous*

70

Exercises

-**ous** is from Latin and means *full of, having to do with, all about.*

What are these **full of** or **all about**?

For example: *She's adventurous* and full of <u>adventure</u>.

1. It's *mountainous* so it's full of _____

2. They're *courageous* so they're full of _____

3. He's *humorous* so he's full of _____

4. It's *mysterious* so it's full of _____

5. *Famous* is all about _____

6. *Glamorous* is all about _____

Change these to their -ous adjective:

danger — _____   nerve — _____

vary — _____   humor — _____

courage — _____   fame — _____

poison — _____   glamour — _____

Put these -ous words in the gaps: *various, famous, nervous.*

He wants to be a _____ musician and play _____

types of music, but he gets very _____ when he plays in

front of his friends.

Answers

1. It's *mountainous* so it's full of <u>mountains</u>.

2. They're *courageous* so they're full of <u>courage</u>.

3. He's *humorous* so he's full of <u>humor</u>.

4. It's *mysterious* so it's full of <u>mystery</u>.

5. *Famous* is all about <u>fame</u>.

6. *Glamorous* is all about <u>glamour</u>.

➜Now write a sentence like this for **nervous, poisonous** and **furious**.

_____

_____

_____

danger — <u>dangerous</u>	nerve — <u>nervous</u>
vary — <u>various</u>	humor — <u>humorous</u>
courage — <u>courageous</u>	fame — <u>famous</u>
poison — <u>poisonous</u>	glamour — <u>glamorous</u>

He wants to be a <u>famous</u> musician and play <u>various</u> types of music, but he gets very <u>nervous</u> when he plays in front of his friends.

➜Write a sentence like this with three of your favorite -ous words. Or write about these two.

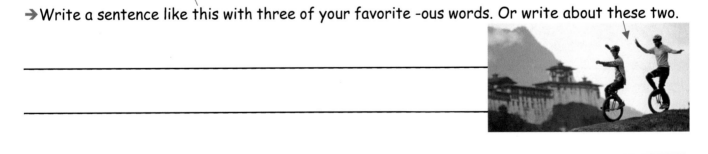

_____

_____

_____

_____

Word Search

This one is tricky — can you do it?

adventurous

dangerous

famous

furious

glamorous

glorious

marvelous

mysterious

nervous

serious

various

```
a s z w j x s t w f m w f v s
t d j a t e e u a r y b c a u
s j v m s d i m o l s n o r o
t e n e r v o u s l t n s i i
g d r e n u k i l d e t m o r
x v s i s t l t a z r v c u o
x x k m o v u n t b i d r s l
o a g a r u g r m v o u h a g
i m g o p e s s o o u s n v m
r e b a r c u w a u s x c g c
i s u o r o m a l g s l y f w
l b u r i c b w p j f p f q n
l s p r z e y z m a p s p a p
w p u u c c d r f o h r z g u
a f w i k p b f s c q i z z j
```

➔1:1:1 doubling up preparation

1. What do these mean? Have a guess. It's fine if you're wrong.

➔Vowel and consonant suffixes

➔Syllables

➔Syllable stress

 It's perfectly OK if you don't know. We're going to look at these next.

The Doubling Up Rules — When and Why

Review of key terms you need for this rule.

→ **Suffixes** are little words we add to the end of a word:
consonant suffixes: *-s, -ment, -ful, -ly, -ness*…
vowel suffixes: *-ing, -ed, -er, -ant, -ance, -ent, -able, -ible*… And *-y* at the end of words.

→ **Syllables** are little spoken chunks with a vowel or vowel sound in it. Read these out loud and slowly: *mom* ("mom"), *happy* ("hap-py"), *probably* ("pro-bab-ly").

Breaking a word into syllables means:
- you break a word down into little spoken chunks,
- each chunk is called a syllable,
- each chunk usually has a vowel or vowel sound in it.

1 syllable: *mom* — "mom"
2 syllables: *happy* — "hap-py"
3 syllables: *unhappy* — "un-hap-py"
4 syllables: *accidental* — "ac-ci-den-tal"
5 syllables: examination — "ex-am-in-a-tion"

👍Breaking a word down into syllables can help you spell a word and remember the prefixes, suffixes and silent letters. "Wed-nes-day", "dis-ap-pear", "Feb-ru-a-ry."

→ **Syllable stress**: When we say words, certain syllables can be stronger than others. Say the following words out loud and notice this: *careful, unhappy, begin, forget, prefer*
First syllable stress: "CAREf-ul"
Second syllable stress: "un-HAP-py"
Last syllable stress, which is important to remember when doubling up longer words: *begin* ("be-GIN"), *forget* ("for-GET"), *occur* ("oc-CUR")… *beginner, forgetting, occurrence*

→Don't worry if syllables and stress are hard for you to hear or figure out; it's no problem. Find words within words to help, or spot the vowels.

The 1:1:1 **doubling up rule (The twinning rule)**

→ Do you know when and why we double up the end consonant in these "little" words?
put — putting, big — bigger, sun — sunny, swim — swimmer, shop — shopped

👍 It's perfectly OK if you don't know. We're going to discover this rule next.

1:1:1 Doubling Up Rule for Little Words

→ **When?** We double up the end consonant with vowel suffixes

big — bigger, sun — sunny, quit — quitting, blur — blurred

→ when we have

1 syllable + **1** vowel next to **1** end consonant

hop

1:1:1

→ **Why?** The double letters indicate a short vowel sound, so we don't get the word mixed up with the magic "e" silent "e" long sound.

long: *hope — hoping*   short: *hop — hopping*

→ Say these words out loud and notice the short and long vowel sounds.

→ We never double up w, x, y, or c.

---

run — running, runny (but not **runs** — only double up with vowel suffixes)

hot — hotter, hottest

sun — sunned, sunning, sunny, sunnier, sunniest

thin — thinner, thinnest, thinned

swim — swimmer, swimming

sit — sitting, sitter, babysitter, babysitting

set — setting, settings, setting-up, setter, settle

big — bigger, biggest, biggish, biggie

sad — sadder, saddest, sadden, saddened

mad — madder, maddest, madden, maddening

*It's very **sunny** so I'm going **swimming**.*

stop — stopper, stopped, stopping, stoppage, unstoppable

slop — slopped, slopping, sloppy, sloppier, sloppiest

fat — fatter, fattest, fatten, fatting, fatty

kid — kiddo, kiddie/kiddy, kidding, kidded

blur — blurred, blurring, blurry

quiz — quizzing, quizzed, quizzes, quizzer, quizzical

whiz — whizzes, whizzed, whizzing, whizzer

*__quit__ —quitting, quitter   *__squat__ — squatting, squatter, squatted

*"q" is always spelled with a "u" in English words, so the "u" is not classed as an extra vowel.

➜ Can you remember why we double up the end consonant?

➜ Look at the pairs of words below. When you read them, you should be able to hear the difference between the short and long vowel sounds.

(hope) hoping vs hopping (hop)
hoped vs hopped

(slime) sliming vs slimming (slim)
slimed vs slimmed

(tape) taping vs tapping (tap)
taped vs tapped

Exercise

Write the root word, vowel sound, and rule.

Word	Root word	Long or short vowel sound	Rule
hoping	hope	long	Drop the "e" with -ing.
hopping	hop	short	1:1:1 doubling up rule.
rating			
ratting			
taped			
tapped			
pining			
pinning			
slimed			
slimmed			
biter			
bitter			

Answers

Word	Root word	Long or short vowel sound	Rule
hoping	hope	long	Drop the "e" with -ing.
hopping	hop	short	1:1:1 doubling up rule.
rating	rate	long	Drop the "e" with -ing.
ratting	rat	short	1:1:1 doubling up rule.
taped	tape	long	Drop the "e" with -ed.
tapped	tap	short	1:1:1 doubling up rule.
pining	pine	long	Drop the "e" with -ing.
pinning	pin	short	1:1:1 doubling up rule.
slimed	slime	long	Drop the "e" with -ed.
slimmed	slim	short	1:1:1 doubling up rule.
biter	bite	long	Drop the "e" with -er.
bitter	bit	short	1:1:1 doubling up rule.

Write a sentence with some of these words.

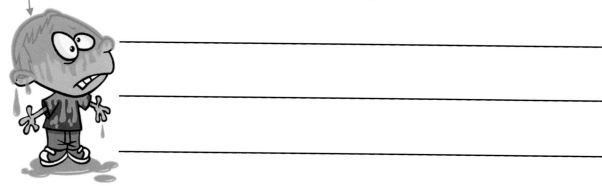

_____

_____

_____

➔ We also double up longer words.

Do you know when we double up and when we don't?

begin — beginner, forget — forgetting, prefer — preferred, but not preference

👍 It's perfectly OK if you don't know. We're going to discover this rule next.

1:1:1 Doubling Up Rule for Longer Words

→ We double up longer words if they end in

1 **vowel** + 1 end consonant and the stress is on the end syllable*:

begin, forget prefer —"beGIN" forGET" "preFER"

We only double up with vowel suffixes.

---

begin ("beGIN") — beginner, beginning (not *begins* because "s" is not a vowel suffix)

forget ("forGET") — forgetting, forgettable/unforgettable

forgot — forgotten

regret — regrettable, regrettably, regretting, regretted

upset — upsetting

forbid — forbidden, forbidding

admit — admitting, admittance, admitted, admittedly

commit — committed, committing, committal, committee

(not *commitment* — consonant suffix)

submit — submitting, submitted

prefer — preferred, preferring (not *preferable*, *preference* — stress on the first syllable)

When the stress isn't on the final syllable, don't double up:

garden ("GARden") — *gardening, gardener*

limit — *limiting, limited, limitation*

*If you can't hear the stress, no problem, see the spelling patterns or use a memory trick.

→ Remember to only double up with vowel suffixes. Compare these:

dropper/droplet, inner/inward, sunny/sunless, strappy/strapless, swimmer/swims
hottest/hotly, goddess/godly, shipping/shipment, redden/redness

→ Remember with longer two-syllable words, double up with a vowel suffix when the stress is on the last syllable. No doubling up with consonant suffixes.

preferred but preference   committed but commitment (consonant suffix)

referring but reference   equipped but equipment (consonant suffix)

beginner but begins (consonant suffix)

Exercise

To double or not to double

Add the suffixes to these root words and double up or not:

Root word	Add -s	Add -ing	Add -ed (or is it an irregular past?)	Add -er, -ment, or -ful if possible
stop	stops	stopping	stopped	stopper
swim			( )	
squat				
admit				
commit				
regret				
begin			( )	
prefer				
quiz				

➜ Remember, we double up longer words:
- with vowel suffixes,
- when the stress is on the last syllable.

➜ If you can't hear the stress, no problem,
  see the spelling patterns or use a memory trick.

VALLEY
OF
FORGOTTEN
PASSWORDS

Answers

To double or not to double

Root word	Add -s	Add -ing	Add -ed (irregular)	Add -er, -ment, or -ful if possible
stop	stops	stopping	stopped	stopper
swim	swims	swimming	(swam)	swimmer
squat	squats	squatting	squatted	squatter
admit	admits	admitting	admitted	_____
commit	commits	committing	committed	commitment
regret	regrets	regretting	regretted	regretful
begin	begins	beginning	(began)	beginner
prefer	prefers	preferring	preferred	_____
quiz	quizzes*	quizzing	quizzed	quizzer

Adding es to words

*We add **es** to words ending in **s**, **ss**, **z**, **x**, **ch**, **sh** to make plurals and third person singular for verbs: *He **washes** the **dishes** and she **watches** the TV. It **crashes** all the time.*
Plural nouns: *She has two **businesses** selling paint **brushes**.*

➜**es** is a vowel suffix so we can use the doubling up rule:

quiz — quizzes, whiz — whizzes have two rules: the 1:1:1 doubling up rule and adding -es rule.

gas — gases	wash — washes	bench — benches	fox — foxes	quiz — quizzes
class — classes	wish — wishes	church — churches	box — boxes	fizz — fizzes
address — addresses	ash — ashes	beach — beaches	fix — fixes	waltz — waltzes
business — businesses	bash — bashes	peach — peaches		

➜Write a sentence with some of these -es words.

Exercise

Which of these are right? Use the 1:1:1 rule or can you see what looks right?

Writing the root word might help.

1. a. shoper (b. shopper) shop

2. a. foxes b. foxxes _____

3. a. beginner b. beginer _____

4. a. fatest b. fattest _____

5. a. sleeping b. sleepping _____

6. a. forgetable b. forgettable _____

7. a. quicker b. quickker _____

8. a. budgetting b. budgeting _____

9. a. quized b. quizzed _____

10. a. appearing b. appearring _____

Remember, spelling only improves if you:
- ➤ study it
- ➤ practice it
- ➤ think about it
- ➤ notice it
- ➤ write it

Word Search

admittance
babysitter
beginner
committee
forbidden
forgotten
preferred
quitter
quizzing
shopping
sunnier
swimming
unforgettable
unstoppable
upsetting

```
d b i n v s m r j s f s e w e
g c a m e u w a e o m e q l d
v s e b i t l i r t t m b f e
b v e y y i t b m t t a n r r
u s v b d s i o i m t i r v r
a h m v x d i m g t i i u o e
d o a e d l m t e r w n s q f
m p o e x o u g t d o a g a e
i p n r c j r v x e r f v r r
t i z e o o q s p a r y h v p
t n o i f g n i t t e s p u u
a g u n s t o p p a b l e q l
n d u n g n i z z i u q d l n
c l u u z b e g i n n e r t m
e q b s w h e u b e i x b a j
```

Answers

1. (shop) a. shoper b. shopper (1:1:1 doubling up rule.)

2. (fox) a. foxes b. foxxes (Add -**es** to "x" rule — never double up "x.")

3. (begin) a. beginner b. beginer (1:1:1 doubling up rule.)

4. (fat) a. fatest b. fattest (1:1:1 doubling up rule.)

5. (sleep) a. sleeping b. sleepping (2 vowels before final consonant so "p" not doubled.)

6. (forget) a. forgetable b. forgettable (1:1:1 doubling up rule.)

7. (quick) a. quicker b. quickker (2 consonants at the end so "k" not doubled.)

8. (budget) a. budgetting b. budgeting (Stress is on the "bud" so "t" not doubled.)

9. (quiz) a. quized b. quizzed (1:1:1 doubling up rule.)

10. (appear) a. appearing b. appearring (2 vowels before end consonant so don't double up.)

82

A Revision Exercise

Warning!

Multiple choice exercises can really mess with your brain because they give you spelling alternatives which also look right!

Multiple choice exercises are only useful when you can use various strategies to help you, such as:

- using memory tricks
- understanding spelling rules
- knowing common letter patterns
- seeing vowels

Which is correct?

1. a. seperate
   b. separate

2. a. sentence
   b. sentance

3. a. address
   b. adress

4. a. beleive
   b. believe

5. a. calender
   b. calendar

6. a. business
   b. buisness

7. a. peculier
   b. peculiar

8. a. argument
   b. arguement

9. a. explosion
   b. explotion

10. a. experiance
    b. experience

11. a. accident
    b. accidant

12. a. disappear
    b. disapear

13. a. disatisfied
    b. dissatisfied

14. a. probabely
    b. probably

15. a. famous
    b. fameous

16. a. naturaly
    b. naturally

17. a. writing
    b. writeing

18. a. truly
    b. truely

19. a. difficalt
    b. difficult

20. a. grammer
    b. grammar

21. a. actualy
    b. actually

22. a. beginer
    b. beginner

23. a. position
    b. posistion

24. a. pressure
    b. presure

Answers on page 85.

Remember, there are lots of ways to improve, learn, and remember your spelling:

Just because you've seen a word once doesn't mean you're going to be able to spell it. You have to work on spelling and study it just like math, art, history, or any other subject. To help, try to:

→ Understand the meaning of the word (use a dictionary).

→ Think of a memory trick, see words within words, **use rhymes** and **sentences** to help spell the word.

→ Do word art — color in the tricky bits and/or the vowels to help you see and remember.

→ Notice the prefixes, suffixes, and **spelling rules**.

→ Write a sentence and draw a picture.

→ Practice and work on your spelling constantly!

Go over this book again. Learning anything well takes a few tries, so keep trying.

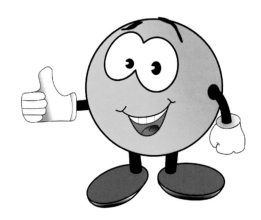

Answers

These are useful words that you'll use, and when you do, I hope this book has given you a trick or two to remember them.

1. a. ~~seperate~~
   b. separate

2. a. sentence
   b. ~~sentance~~

3. a. address
   b. ~~adress~~

4. a. ~~beleive~~
   b. believe

5. a. ~~calender~~
   b. calendar

6. a. business
   b. ~~buisness~~

7. a. ~~peculier~~
   b. peculiar

8. a. argument
   b. ~~arguement~~

9. a. explosion
   b. ~~explotion~~

10. a. ~~experiance~~
    b. experience

11. a. accident
    b. ~~accidant~~

12. a. disappear
    b. ~~disapear~~

13. a. ~~disatisfied~~
    b. dissatisfied

14. a. ~~probabely~~
    b. probably

15. a. famous
    b. ~~fameous~~

16. a. ~~naturaly~~
    b. naturally

17. a. writing
    b. ~~writeing~~

18. a. truly
    b. ~~truely~~

19. a. ~~difficalt~~
    b. difficult

20. a. ~~grammer~~
    b. grammar

21. a. ~~actualy~~
    b. actually

22. a. ~~beginer~~
    b. beginner

23. a. position
    b. ~~posistion~~

24. a. pressure
    b. ~~presure~~

→ I know this type of exercise is not as hard as spelling the words in a spelling test or writing, so that's why it's important to use these words in a piece of writing, or get your friend to give you a spelling test, or write a story together.

→ What did you get wrong? A letter, the rule? By studying your mistakes, you can figure out how to remember the spelling next time. Don't forget to use memory tricks to help, and other spelling strategies you like.

These are the words I need to work on.

Congratulations – you're a star!

Give yourself a big pat on the back and a gold medal for finishing.

Keep on enjoying and loving spelling,
Joanne

A Bit About Me

I've been a teacher, lecturer, and teacher trainer for 23 years and have written numerous books and online courses on spelling, punctuation and the history of spelling. I'm the owner of the spelling website, www.howtospell.co.uk.

My Books
For Kids

Spelling Patterns and Rules for 5th Graders: To learn, improve & have fun with spelling (For American English)

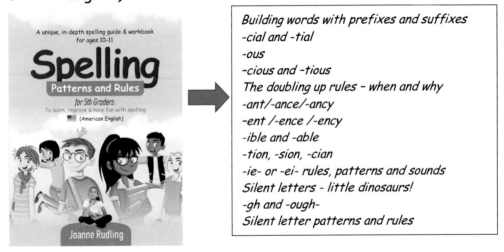

Building words with prefixes and suffixes
-cial and -tial
-ous
-cious and –tious
The doubling up rules – when and why
-ant/-ance/-ancy
-ent /-ence /-ency
-ible and -able
-tion, -sion, -cian
-ie- or -ei- rules, patterns and sounds
Silent letters - little dinosaurs!
-gh and -ough-
Silent letter patterns and rules

Spelling Rules and Patterns for Ages 10-11: To learn, improve & have fun with spelling and writing (For British English)

For Adults (ideal for both American and British English)
Spelling Rules Workbook — a step-by-step guide to the rules of English spelling
Spelling Strategies & Secrets: the essential spelling guide
How to Spell the 20 Most Commonly Misspelled Words
Punctuation Guide and Workbook
The Reasons Why English Spelling is so Weird and Wonderful

Made in the USA
Coppell, TX
25 August 2021